Caring for Exotic Animals

Varunika Ruwanpura

CONTENTS

Who Cares for Exotic Animals?	2
The Snake Handler	4
The Orang-utan Carer	12
The Whale Rescuer	22
Becoming a Carer for Exotic Animals	29
Exotic Animals Quiz	30
Glossary	32

WHO CARES FOR EXOTIC ANIMALS?

Do you look after a pet dog, fish or a rabbit? If you said "yes", then you are an animal carer!

Exotic animal carers must do special training so they know how to care for these animals.

Let's see what a working day is like for three different **exotic** animal carers.

This exotic animal carer looks after tigers.

THE SNAKE HANDLER

Imagine being a snake handler. Sounds dangerous! But snake handlers know all about snakes and other **reptiles**. Most snake handlers work at zoos.

Here's a snake handler with one of the largest snakes in the world – a python.

There are about 6000 different kinds of reptiles in the world. Snakes, tortoises, lizards and crocodiles are all reptiles.

Meet Some Snakes

Snake handlers look after many kinds of snakes, such as cobras, pythons and tree snakes.

King cobras are very **venomous**. One bite could kill a snake handler. So a snake handler must be very careful when holding this snake.

King cobras are from Asia or south-east Asia.

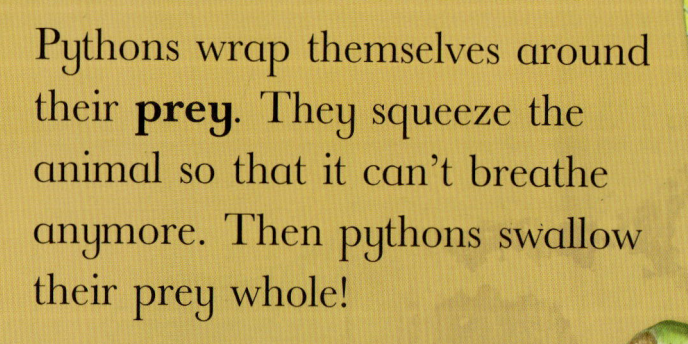

Pythons wrap themselves around their **prey**. They squeeze the animal so that it can't breathe anymore. Then pythons swallow their prey whole!

African tree snakes are small and shy and not dangerous to people. They come out at night to eat lizards and tree frogs.

African tree snakes hide during the day.

Snake Homes

Snake handlers look after the snake cages.

Cobras like lots of leaves to hide under. Pythons like thick grass and rocks to rub against. All snakes like to curl up inside hollow logs.

tree branches

thick shrubs

pond

soil

rocks

Keeping Warm

Snakes are cold-blooded. This means they can't make their own heat to warm their bodies. In the wild, snakes get warm by lying in the sun or on warm rocks.

In a zoo, the snake handler heats their cages with special heat lights.

Snakes stretch out to warm their bodies. Then they curl up quickly to stay warm.

heat lights

Cleaning Up

Snake handlers also have to clean the snake cages. First, they put the snake in another cage or in a large bucket.

Then the snake handler picks up all the rotten leaves and snake poo in the cage.

The snake handler uses a long hook to pick up this rattlesnake gently.

What's for Lunch?

Another job is feeding the snakes. In the wild, snakes eat mice, rats, chicks, lizards and even other snakes. So, they need to eat the same food as they would eat in the wild.

Snakes don't chew their food. They eat it whole. The pictures below show an anaconda eating a large rodent.

The snake opens its mouth very, very wide.

It swallows its food whole.

An anaconda is one of the biggest snakes in the world. It can sometimes last on one meal for a year! But it has to be a very big meal such as a deer or a large rodent.

This viper snake is eating a mouse.

A bump can be seen going down the snake's body.

The food is broken down inside the snake.

11

THE ORANG-UTAN CARER

How would you like to look after baby orang-utans? That's what orang-utan carers do at this Malaysian wildlife park. Some baby orang-utans in the wildlife park are only a few weeks old. They need lots of cuddles!

The word "orang-utan" means "man of the forest" in the Malay language.

The Great Apes

orang-utan

gorilla

chimpanzee

Orang-utans, gorillas and chimpanzees are all great apes.

Where's Mum?

All the orang-utans at this wildlife park are orphans. This means they've lost their mothers. When people cut down **rainforests**, orang-utans lose their homes.

Many rainforest trees are cut down for farming.

A wildlife worker cares for a baby orang-utan at the wildlife park.

A Vet Check

When a baby orang-utan arrives at the wildlife park, a **vet** checks for any illnesses.

This baby orang-utan will join other orang-utans when it is well.

At the park, there is an animal hospital. There is also a special room where the animals stay until they are well again. They can then join the other orang-utans.

Indoor and Outdoor Nursery

Looking after baby orang-utans is a twenty-four-hour job. Babies sleep and play in a **nursery** until they are four years old.

Like human babies, they cry for milk day and night. The carers feed them lots of bottles of milk.

Forest School

When the orang-utans are old enough, they go to "forest school". They learn to:
- pick fruit
- climb trees
- make a nest with leaves.

Carers teach baby orang-utans the things that wild orang-utans learn from their mums!

Going Home

Slowly, the orang-utans learn to do things by themselves. Then carers let the orang-utans go back into the forest where they can live without help.

Saying goodbye is sad but the forest is the orang-utans' real home.

THE WHALE RESCUER

Whale rescuers work in a group. They look after whales that get sick or injured.

Whales can get injured if they get caught up in fishing nets.

Sometimes, whales end up on beaches. Whales are so big and heavy that they can't move back out to the sea by themselves. So the whale rescue group tries to help them.

Being a Whale Rescuer

Whale rescue groups get reports when a whale is injured at sea or on land. Then they rush to the whale to try and help it.

net

Divers help a whale caught in a net.

If a whale is caught in a fishing net, people from the group will put on their scuba gear and jump into the sea. They will cut the nets to free the whale.

Saving Whales on the Beach

When whales gets stuck on the beach, a vet from the whale rescue group checks the health of the whales.

Whale rescuers pour water on the whales to make sure they stay wet and cold. Then the group use special equipment to move the whales back out to sea.

This whale is being picked up in a sling and will be taken back out to sea.

Out to Sea

The aim of the whale rescue group is to make sure a whale is free and healthy.

Whales breathe out of blowholes on top of their heads. Whales can stay under water for a long time, about twenty minutes, but they do need to rise above the water to breathe.

BECOMING A CARER FOR EXOTIC ANIMALS

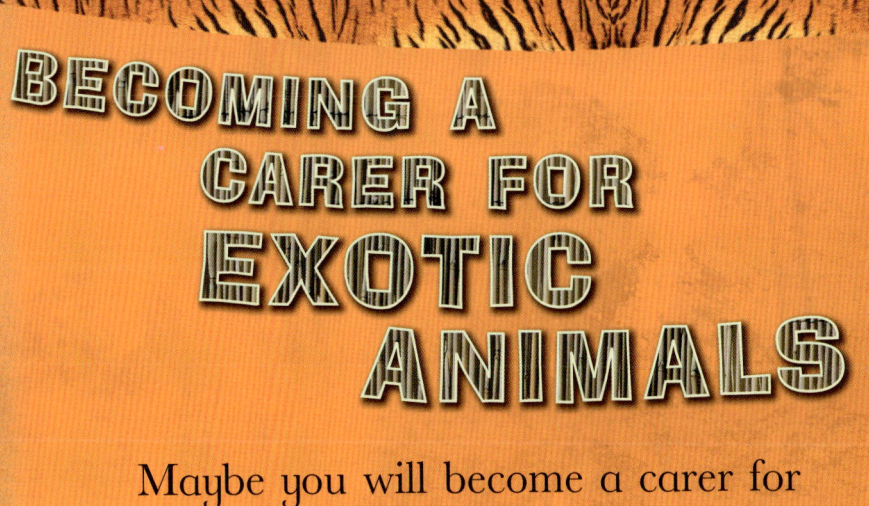

Maybe you will become a carer for exotic animals one day.

Here's how to start:
- Volunteer at a zoo.
- Join a wildlife rescue group.
- You can also study to be an animal scientist.

Feeding a hippopotamus

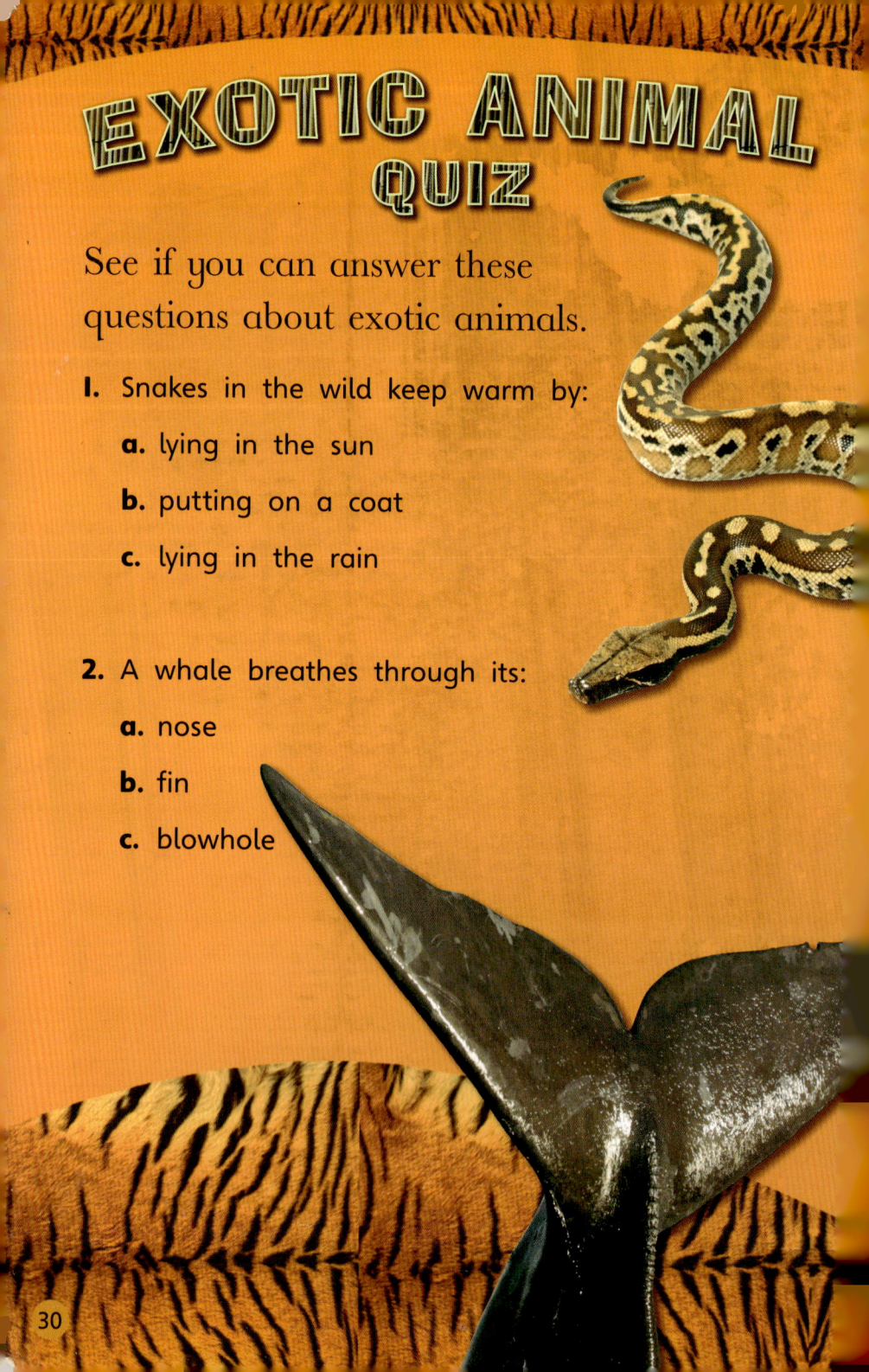

EXOTIC ANIMAL QUIZ

See if you can answer these questions about exotic animals.

1. Snakes in the wild keep warm by:
   a. lying in the sun
   b. putting on a coat
   c. lying in the rain

2. A whale breathes through its:
   a. nose
   b. fin
   c. blowhole

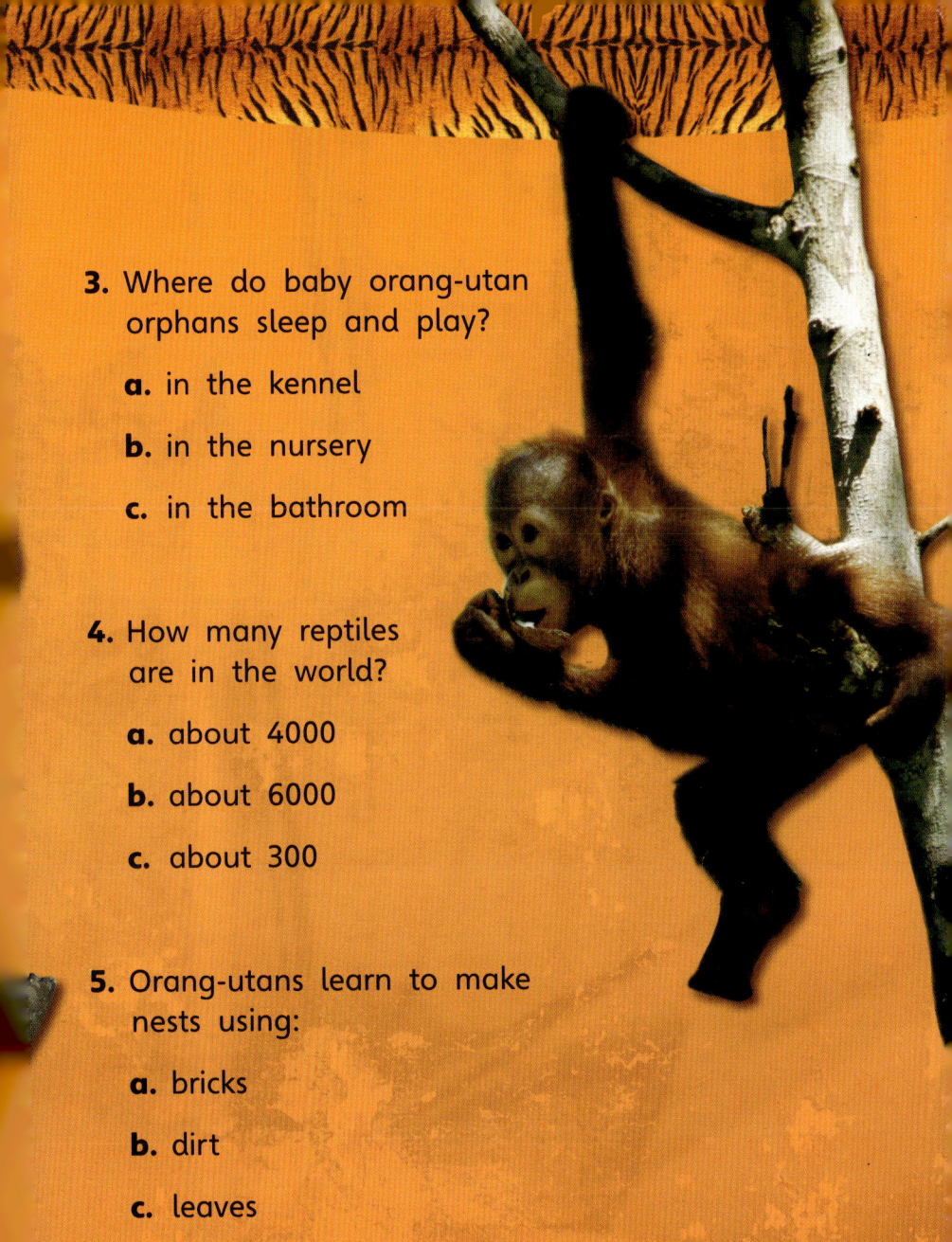

3. Where do baby orang-utan orphans sleep and play?

    a. in the kennel

    b. in the nursery

    c. in the bathroom

4. How many reptiles are in the world?

    a. about 4000

    b. about 6000

    c. about 300

5. Orang-utans learn to make nests using:

    a. bricks

    b. dirt

    c. leaves

Answers

1. a 2. c 3. b 4. b 5. c

GLOSSARY

exotic from another country

nursery room where babies sleep and play

prey animal killed by another animal for food

rainforests forests with a high amount of rainfall

reptiles cold-blooded animals, such as tortoises, snakes or crocodiles, that have an outer covering of scales or plates and lay eggs

venomous poisonous

vet animal doctor